Mind You Eat Your Vegetables!™

Moms Who Get It...and Max

Sydney Ashland

Pam Simon, M.S.W.

Max Fickas

Fidgets2WidgetsPublishing™, Oregon

CONTENTS

Acknowledgements

First and foremost we would like to acknowledge the gift of Mojang and specifically, the brilliance of Markus Persson. Minecraft has changed 21st century childhood forever. Thank you.

Secondly, we want to thank George Brown for the gift of his wisdom. Not only was he one of our very first, joyful, curious Widgetarians™, but he was the first to bring Minecraft to Fidgets2Widgets.

Finally, we want to thank those like-minded visionaries who have inspired and believed in us. Where would we be without our weekly visits from Senior Widgetarian, Julian Farrand; our rocks, sand dollars and visits from nature guru, Jean Nesta-Berry; the support of therapist and advisory board member, Paula Prober; the brainstorming sessions with Stephen Fickas, et al.; the insight and complete understanding of our vision from Deborah Garlin; and all the elbow grease and muscle power of the many supporters who helped prepare our physical space and shared resources? A huge thank you to Jay Stuart, Barb Stuart, Harriet Simon and all our other family members and friends.

Introduction

Frustrated with the lack of afterschool options for her son as he moved through elementary and into middle school, Sydney Ashland, entrepreneur, began thinking about alternatives. Noticing that test anxiety and large classroom environments were negatively impacting her son's performance at school, Sydney researched alternative schooling as well as afterschool programs. Months later, having found very few options, she decided to homeschool her son. A lover of technology and strong proponent of the digital age, she wanted to make sure her son was prepared for the ever evolving digital economy. Sydney started curating and creating curriculum herself.

As Sydney's passion and exuberance grew, she began to see a business opportunity. Her vision began to expand to include offering a formalized program for others. In 2012 she collaborated with Pam Simon, mother and M.S.W., to co-found Fidgets2Widgets (F2W). F2W is a boredom-free zone where kids ages 9-14 use cutting edge technology to enrich their lives in a holistic afterschool environment. Eugene, Oregon was the perfect technology-rich location for this enrichment program.

Co-founder, Pam Simon, with a background in speech pathology and social work, uses her expertise in ongoing program development, helping to create a healthy nurturing environment for kids (Widgetarians) and their families.

The vision for F2W was to create a technology Center for late elementary and middle school kids. This casual learning Center would provide daily homework help, daily learning modules with weekly themes. Technology would be available to all. Little did we know at the time, that Minecraft would be a such a perfect and major teaching tool. Of course we would use other web based tools too, but Minecraft has been a game changer. Every part of this vision has been realized and more.

Since its inception, F2W has served over 400 children from 35 schools in Lane County.

Something all these kids share, is a LOVE of

Minecraft!

CHAPTER 1

"I just don't get it..."

That's what they said about skateboarding, fast food and reality television. Minecraft is no longer a phenomenon. It is a childhood reality that is here to stay like Disney and Lego. Minecraft enhances a child's ability to play and pretend. Like Lego, it provides a platform where creativity expands into infinity.

This generation of children move seamlessly between the digital and physical worlds. Children are used to playing on cell phones, tablets, gaming consoles like Wii-U and X-Box Kinect, then minutes later, they are outside playing with friends or in team sports.

These authors grew up with the admonition, "Mind your manners," only to hear ourselves saying years later, "Mind yourself on Minecraft! No griefing or trolling and by all means, know who you are playing with!" The more things change, the more they stay the same! Kids still need guidance and soft nudges to play nice; it's merely the context that has changed.

"Who has obsidian?" Phil typed quickly. "I can trade many specialty items." I watched him type and was impressed with his speed, as he was only 10 years-old at the time. He chortled excitedly when someone responded positively and the trade was made. Another player dropped obsidian blocks and Phil quickly gathered them for his next build, a stadium that was going to be EPIC!

Imagine using digitalized blocks of wood that you have chopped to build a home. And as you build your home, you realize that the blocks of wood you have chopped are not enough! You want windows, flooring, beautiful lighting fixtures. You want to create your very own kitchen. You want a wood table and chairs. The excitement builds. How can you accumulate materials to build all of these items? You quickly ask your closest friend for help and they rapidly recite all the items you will need to create the house of your dreams. Welcome to Minecraft. You are well on your way… Oh, and did we mention the close friend you turned to for advice lives across several states and yet was more easily accessed than your neighbor next door?

Max, our Chief Gaming Officer and Minecraft Expert, shares some of his thoughts…

There are hundreds of Minecraft items and every one has a use. Some kids are walking encyclopedias filled with Minecraft information. Others, barely scratch the surface in a year of playing. They are all left with a lasting sense of discovery as they are constantly learning new ways of play in the game. The kids form their own economy without even realizing it. They assign value to items based on Supply and Demand. A watermelon isn't worth as much as a diamond, but if you're in the mining business

and in desperate need of food, you might just make that trade. It's a free market system.

As television, cell phones and computers have become commonplace across the globe, the applications each of these devices use have grown exponentially. And as the applications and software programs expand, so does our vocabulary. We use Widgets on our cell phones to schedule our days, track our exercise, and store phone numbers. Evening activities are no longer influenced by T.V. programming, we just record or stream our favorite shows. And computers are no longer relegated to our workplaces. We use our phones for everything. We speak of "Googling," a commonplace activity that never existed 30 years ago. The Information

Age has changed how we think and how we speak. It has also influenced how we play.

Playing has been replaced in large part by the concepts of gaming. Pretending of years ago where "house" or "school" was imitated, now is referred to as RPG or Role Play Gaming. The Information Age has moved into our culture so rapidly, many of us have been taken totally unaware. Before we knew it our cars had keyless entries and now start without a key. Our refrigerators and stoves and sprinkler systems are all "smart." So are our CHILDREN!

"Oh, and another thing," Max circles back to where we are writing. "Kids have been Role Playing since the beginning of time. It is the act of taking on a role or character and 'pretending'

to be that character. Girls playing 'house,' boys playing 'cops and robbers,' are the classic stereotypes, but now you just might find the roles reversed. RPers like a challenge."

Give any three-year-old your cell phone and they will unlock pictures and find free games faster than you can. Generate an online world where anything can be created and you have given your child the keys to the kingdom of make-believe. Minecraft is just such a world. In this game you "mine" resources and create or "craft" items. It is based on reality to such a degree that you can cut grass, plow, plant seeds, build structures, practice and learn engineering concepts with pulleys and levers and pressure plates. You can create magic potions, increase your vitality and life through healthy

14

eating, face scary enemies like large spiders and spindly skeletons or creepers. All this barely scratches the surface of Minecraft.

Minecraft is known as a Sandbox Game. You are dropped into the wilderness with nothing and you must make it on your own. There's nothing telling you what to do or where to go. Like playing in a sandbox in your backyard, you make your own fun, your imagination being the limit. The sense of exploration and discovery is immense in a game like this.

And it is a game played in community. Open your world to LAN (Local Area Network) or go on a Minecraft Server and all of your friends can help you build whatever your heart desires. Cooperation and competition are the social building blocks of Minecraft. This is a game that socializes, teaches and expands your child's world.

We recently observed a child from Germany playing Minecraft with a group of 30 American children. They did not speak each other's national language, but they ALL spoke the language of Minecraft. A railroad was built in total cooperation with squeals of laughter and jabbering in English and German. No one was self-conscious or inhibited. And so much was learned.

Because the virtual world of Minecraft is so fabulous and fantastical, children don't want to LEAVE their play. What parents don't understand is that this is not a game of winning or losing. This is a game of pure creativity. It would be like interrupting your child in the middle of a Lego set build or tree house in the back yard. Only in the Minecraft world, you can obtain items through determination and hard work that you could never obtain in the physical world. Hence, the reluctance of children to leave a world of mining diamonds, swimming in the depths of the sea with squid, or climbing virtual world volcanoes and finding treasures in its depths. And, like reading a good book, time is suspended as you become lost in your play. The magical world of Minecraft is one that we can safely embrace, even enter on our own as adults, if we *dare*.

Just as parents sought to influence their children's play in the past, be it through sports, board games or group activities, it is time we enter the world of Minecraft in order to have just such an influence today. Sports, board games and group activities are still important, but so is Minecraft!

Samuel was a builder extraordinaire in the game. He fashioned homes that left other players coveting his world. One day, during a learning themed activity at our Center (build your own business week), he got the bright idea that he could become a

real estate mogul and sure enough, he couldn't sell his houses fast enough. Another child, Colleen, decided she was going to build a bacon factory. She ingeniously

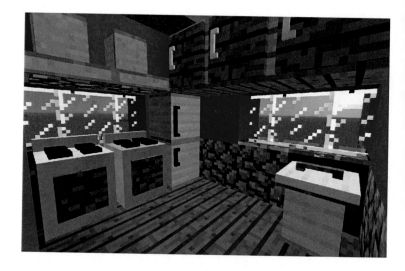

created a humane slaughter house where the pigs transformed quickly into bacon (her favorite food at the time) and then she sold the bacon in the marketplace.

Another child built a bakery where community members were required to grow wheat, raise and milk cows, chickens for eggs, etc. She would buy the ingredients necessary to craft cake and then sell cakes in the marketplace. Ingenuity, creativity and elbow grease, attributes of all three children. Max says, "I want me some bacon!"

The kids pipe in, "Me too, yeah! I want bacon."[1]

---

[1] Every screenshot depicted in this book is an original Minecraft picture created by kids at Fidgets2Widgets.

Wise adults, enrichment and school programs can all use this most wonderful game to educate and inspire kids. This is not a game to be feared. We can trust our children here. Despite the prevalence of first person shooter games and violence run amuck, our children are clamoring in the millions for the experience of a world where they can have free rein with their imaginations, where they can tackle the real world problems on the screen first, where they can learn to work together toward a common end.

CHAPTER 2
"Now I get it. Tell me more..."

All of Danielle's friends were talking about
Minecraft at school. Over time, she became curious.
Danielle's first experience of Minecraft was a
YouTube video. It was a parody, a popular song
reworked to fit a Minecraft theme. The graphics
were beautiful and the song captivating. She was
hooked. From there she went to a Minecraft tutorial
series. She learned everything she could. Danielle
represents the first generation of children who turn
to YouTube as their primary source of information.
Today she is an avid Minecraft enthusiast and
leader of her peer group. Self-taught and Peer
Mentoring are two credible learning methods in

2015. More and more children are learning in online education models. Many parents are comfortable with self-paced, self-initiated models of learning.

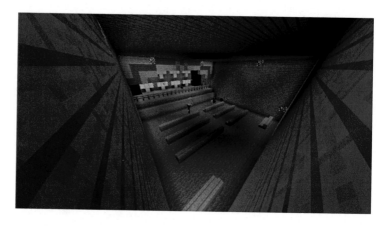

Leadership within this model looks different than a decade ago. Children today have a strong sense of self and because of that assume the responsibility of collaboration, competition, conflict resolution and leadership with much greater ease and at younger ages. Minecraft provides a perfect opportunity to practice and hone these skills. We have repeatedly seen children who were introverted or socially awkward rise to the rank of leader within gameplay. And because there are so many ways in which individual creativity can be expressed, leadership roles shift depending on the activity or challenge of the moment.

Conflict can most certainly be present within the game. There is a fine line between competition and collaboration. Because the game has two play settings of "survival" or "creative" it is relatively easy as the adult to help make positive choices. In the afterschool and educational environments, all participants are encouraged to play in "creative" mode when collaborating and "survival" mode when needing greater challenges or desiring to play competitively. In "creative" mode you get to maintain your inventory (resources you have accumulated) even if you lose health and leave the game. In "survival" mode losing health can mean death and losing your inventory. That being said, on more than one occasion, we have seen a child reach out to another with gifts of inventory when losses are experienced unexpectedly.

You are able to use TNT and other resources (fire, water, air) to destroy or blow-up buildings in either game play mode. Some kids are thrilled when they can build a structure and then "boom" watch it evaporate into space after well placed TNT is detonated. It is not unlike Jenga or wooden blocks at home on your kitchen table. A spawned tornado, flood or fire moves through the structure more slowly. Build a tower and then knock it down with squeals of joy and start again. The role for discerning parents is to identify when the urge to construct or destruct is innocent fun, and when it is hurtful or disrespectful.

One of the terms that kids use within the game to identify someone who is being negatively destructive is called, "griefing." It is very common to hear a child call out, "No griefing! Leave my house please." We love the fact that they have taken a noun and made it a verb, an action word. Being destructive to someone else's property in the game of Minecraft can cause the property owner to feel grief. Someone, somewhere, began using the term as a verb and it has taken off and become part of the Minecraft culture. At our Center we have rules like: "No griefing, No trolling (following people about annoyingly or stalking), no guns, no name calling or cussing, no public servers."

There are many public servers with thousands of players in various worlds or arenas playing Minecraft. Most children have experienced various servers and have their favorites. It is important for parents to know about these servers and observe play within these realms. Some attract the younger set and are pretty creative, fun, enjoyable. Others attract late teens and young adults and can include

chats with pretty colorful language. We discourage
public servers at our Center for just that reason, but
also because we want the children to play with each
other. We encourage parents to get involved and
determine which servers feel comfortable at home.

Most classic video games require that you take on
the "energy" or mindset of the game prior to play.
In order to have your "head" in the game, you must
gear up. Minecraft is different. It is a natural biome
with many differing tasks, exploration opportunities
and group and solitary activities. You need not
change your mindset or mood to get in the game.
You can merely join the game and choose an
activity that fits YOU best. We have seen many
children enter the game feeling quiet, withdrawn or
otherwise muted. Then, at another time, exploring a

new environment or experiencing the victory of a task completed well with others, is exactly what is needed and works as well.

Matthew had worked very hard to tame his wolf on the game and it became his constant companion. Various animals can be tamed on Minecraft. Ocelots become tamed kitties, wolves become dog-like companions, wild horses are tamed into loyal steeds. The children love this aspect of the game. Taming an animal takes patience. There are various tasks you must do to earn an animal's trust and eventually become bonded with each other. Another function of the game is that animals can be quickly killed (no blood and guts) for food or for functional items. Leather, rope, hides are all animal by-products.

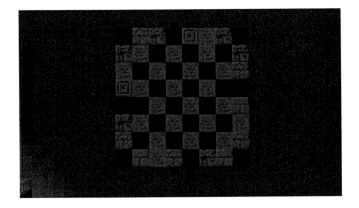

Matthew had patiently worked to earn the trust of his wolf-dog. Another player, happened upon Matthew's wolf and killed it. Matthew, who had developed a bond with this animal, burst into tears. The other child was immediately penitent, mortified at what he had innocently done. Minecraft play stopped and everyone acknowledged their part, their feelings. Grief was shared, remorse was felt, forgiveness was bestowed. It was an amazingly poignant and emotional afternoon at our Center and profound lessons were learned by all. Even those who weren't involved, witnessed the interaction and the ensuing healing process. Minecraft provides just such opportunities for conscience building and social responsibility through the natural consequences inherent in the game.

CHAPTER 3

Fairy Tales, Myths and Math

From "Lions and Tigers and Bears! Oh my!" in the Wizard of OZ, to Grimm's Fairy Tales to, Where the Wild Things Are, we continue to use metaphor and myth to influence character development in our children. The hero's journey is a standard underpinning of many modern-day cultures. Minecraft uses these metaphors beautifully. The monsters are not so truly scary, but provide enough conflict and adversity to make the game play challenging. You may encounter a green creeper, a giant spider, a skeleton, an Enderman, a silver fish deep within the earth, an Enderdragon or a green slime, all monsters within the game.

Creatures in Minecraft are universally known as 'Mobs'. Not all Mobs are hostile, like Chickens or Villagers. If Hostile Mobs are becoming a problem you can change the Difficulty to Peaceful and they will stop appearing. This offers a more relaxed playstyle.

Creepers are nocturnal and enjoy coming out at night to steal blocks and otherwise create havoc. There are ways to mitigate the damage and protect yourself, but it requires a level of problem solving and vigilance that helps reinforce personal responsibility. Just as leaving your bike out in the rain at home might result in a rusty chain, leaving

your "construction site" or home unattended at

night could leave you vulnerable to nocturnal

mischief makers in Minecraft.

The many monsters can be relatively benign and

only attack when provoked, like zombie pigmen or

spiders.

If you can't get enough of the Day in Minecraft, you can actually stop the passing of time using a Command. In the Chat Window, type:

/gamerule DoDayNightCycle False

Now the Days will last forever. Simple change 'False' to 'True' to bring Night back.

The big bad wolf in fairy tales may huff and puff and blow your house down. The troll under the bridge demands his rightful due, so the Minecraft monsters test your fortitude and leave you ever the wiser.

There is another dimension to the game known as the Nether. Its name comes from combining the word "ethers" with the concept of "nowhere."

Hence, the "Nether." You can only reach the Nether through a portal. Within this underworld there are lava springs and fire, as well as unique items that can't be found anywhere else. Glowstone is a commodity from this region that can be transported back through the portal and used in creative mode, as can bedrock and gravel. This region is filled with unique monsters and universal archetypes. Kids love to travel the nether to experience the hot lava, the challenge of staying alive amidst the many pitfalls and dangers. They can participate in the same magic that has animated our fairy tales and myths for centuries. And if they should slip and fall to their deaths, no worries, they return to the overworld unscathed and ready to play some more.

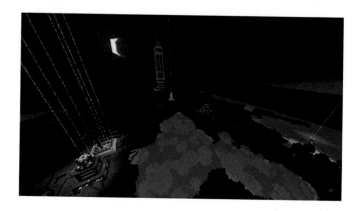

Steve, the main Minecraft character, is the hero of the game. He wanders out into the wilderness with no resources, no instructions, just his good wits and handsome blockage profile. You can change his "skin," otherwise known as clothing in the physical world. Much like Joseph Campbell's description of the Hero's Journey, Steve must deal with the known and unknown. There is a call to adventure with challenges and temptations along the way. Transformation is a natural result of these experiences and the weary traveler returns home wiser, even reborn. True to the tenants of myth where there is a hero and a nemesis, modern day folklore has created Herobrine, a mythical adversary that eludes the most experienced Minecraft player. Herobrine looks like Steve, but has vacant eyes and a robotic personality. No one has ever seen Herobrine in the game, but the players have long believed some of the urban legends, hoping for an appearance only for them. We have often heard kids excitedly report a sighting of the elusive Herobrine much to their fellow player's disbelief. Some wise modders have created versions where Herobrine does exist and YouTube is filled with short videos perpetuating the mystique around this non-existent character. Much like the Lochness

Monster or Sasquatch, players don't really believe

in his existence, but it does add some good natured

fear.

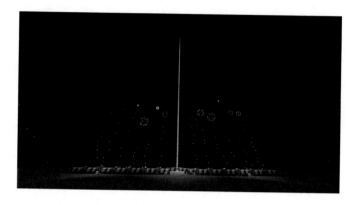

Within Minecraft there are potions and

enchantments that increase or decrease health and

give you special powers. You must have access to

the mathematical formula or secret ingredients to

craft these potions. Speaking of math, in case you

haven't figured it out by now, math is a critical

aspect of the game. No building takes place without

counting blocks, learning how to create symmetry

and balance. As you gain experience, you

accumulate wealth and resources. You must keep

track of these valuable items in order to protect your

health and trade with other players.

Just as math is used in various building, Redstone is

used to power mechanisms like pistons and levers.

Math and engineering are both concepts at work in

this game.

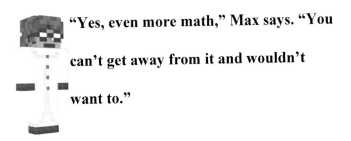 **"Yes, even more math," Max says. "You can't get away from it and wouldn't want to."**

Children become adept at calculating in their heads.

Yet, we often find scraps of paper with coordinates,

math computations or positive and negative electrical formulas strewn around the computer rooms. In this context, math is fun and engineering is far from daunting.

Crafting recipes are quite specific and will only work with precise measurements. The same is true for command blocks and in game chat. Precision when describing what unique items you need or when reporting your exact location is a must. Your friends could easily find themselves in the wilderness or ocean if you miscalculate your location. As you move through the game, you have access to a compass at all times. You learn to read maps and are aware of your coordinates. Geography within Minecraft is ever changing and worth memorizing, for you never know when you might need to retrace your steps and increase your

experience enroute.

CHAPTER 4

A Leap of Faith and Minecraft Education

Fidgets2Widgets is a brick and mortar after school enrichment program where kids, ages 9-14, socialize, learn through Minecraft, are taught to code, exercise with Fitbits and explore the concepts of Science, Technology, Engineering and Math (STEM). Over 400 children from 35 schools in an Oregon city of 200, 000 have attended Minecraft Club on Saturday, an After School Enrichment Module or Summer Camp. Following is excerpted from <u>After School Today</u>, the National Afterschool Association Magazine.

"Fidgets2Widgets is a welcoming environment where everyone is comfortable. Kids who self-identify as geeks or nerds, social kids, kids who may struggle with Asperger's or mild autism, kids who are gifted—they all get along and form relationships. No cliques. No bullying. They are all Widgetarians!"says Pam Simon co-owner. Yet the Fidgets2Widgets concept came primarily from a collaborative relationship with co-founder Sydney Ashland. Their real education was in raising their own children. "We saw a big disconnect between school life during the day and digital/virtual life at night on computers, tablets, phones, and gaming consoles," said Simon. Digital/virtual life was social, relevant, current, and engaging in a way school wasn't. Social media, gaming, and texting became the modern-day playground. Technology is the language children speak; the way in. Although children in general think they know everything technologically, Simon and Ashland saw the need for close supervision and guidance regarding safety, discernment, balance, and skills—tools not taught with great prevalence in schools. And afterschool enrichment options become very limited closer to middle school. Children were no longer satisfied with afterschool care that felt more like "babysitting." Rather than continuing to complain about what didn't exist, Simon and Ashland took a huge leap of faith and built a concept, program, and casual learning environment centered on what they'd observed. They leased physical space, ordered furniture and devices, and began creating the curriculum to support their tag line: "Holistic, High Energy, High Tech." They wanted a casual learning environment where fully engaged children experience technology through the "active creator" (not "passive user") lens. They constantly survey the children to see what they are interested in learning. One example was integrating Minecraft and other educational gaming platforms into their learning modules. As a social worker, Simon's basic tenet is, "meet the client where he/she is." She and Ashland know that to reach their digital natives, they must meet them at technology—their love and way of life. "As long as we are in charge, supervising, structuring, and mentoring, we know they are using technology in appropriate ways." Fidgets2Widgets has a structure children relate to and use as a container of exploration. Children are mastering basic STEM skills, and because the environment is relaxed and holistic, they move freely from exercise bike to balance board to Legos to Wii to computers. "When it's time to meet as a group and tackle the learning module for the day, there is exuberance, joy, and great social interaction." Simon and Ashland relate to the children as female role models and mentors, with that nurturing "mom" energy thrown in for good measure. "We are middle-age women who love technology ourselves," said Simon. She and Ashland are committed to remaining on the cutting edge and helping children experience technology. "We find ourselves staying one step ahead of the kids. It can be daunting at times, but as lifelong nerds ourselves, we enjoy it!" •*Leap of Faith, After*

School Today Magazine•Winter2015

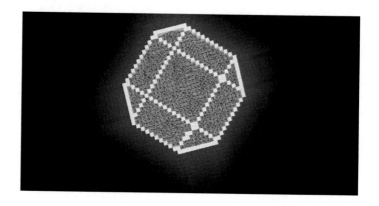

Ben carefully counted blocks as he created a

complex beehive complete with honeycomb. His

friends patiently waited outside the hive for a "tour"

of the inside. The honeycomb was magnificent and

multi colored. There were accommodations inside

the hive for beekeepers and bees alike. We were

studying the concept of fibonacci and geometric

design. In our Minecraft Module, hexagons were

used by the children, integrating math skills to place blocks perfectly as they designed elaborate constructs. It wasn't about getting it perfect or being graded, it was about the pure satisfaction and joy of creating and sharing while learning the basics, something we do at F2W all of the time. We introduce concepts and then build on them.

Not only do we explore these concepts in Minecraft, but we study the physical world as well. When studying the fibonacci sequence, we examined pinecones, seashells, pineapples and other natural

world items. When studying bees, we had a local beekeeper bring a honeycomb and walked our garden looking for bees. This generation of children is really the first generation to move seamlessly between the digital and physical worlds.

We have used Minecraft to experience various nature biomes, using bug mods and tropical modded editions of the game. The virtual world taps into imagination and curiosity that expands children's concepts about what is possible and/or probable. Playing in a virtual world with large prehistoric and modern day bugs is the perfect bridge for a visit from a local Entomologist with hundreds of specimens. And children move between the worlds, naturally curious in each, uninhibited and excited to learn!

Topics explored at F2W have included architecture and interior design where concepts of size, scale and proportion were taught. In Minecraft, a Furniture Mod was used. Other online tools (Architect Studio 3D and Frank Lloyd Wright) allowed Widgetarians to redesign the F2W space with the help of a local interior design expert.

Towncraft allows children to build small cities that include commercial and personal Real Estate. They build businesses and then operate them using entrepreneurial and business theories. We have built bridges, introducing concepts of mechanical and structural engineering. Kids have opened pet stores, built shipyards and competed during "inventions week" to come up with the best invention. Children were assigned design teams and took their inventions very seriously! We have explored electrical engineering concepts using redstone. We have constructed hydroelectric plants, elevators and generators. We have built railroads and

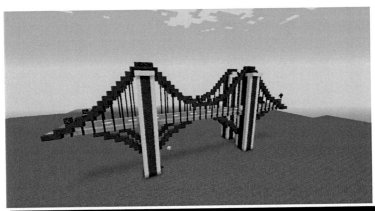

rollercoasters, banks and hotels. Every one of these

learning modules enhanced by the Minecraft

experience..

While the kids are engaged in these creative tasks,

they are extremely focused. They are working while

playing, learning without fear of making mistakes.

A byproduct of Minecraft Education is reading, writing and typing. Skills are practiced through reading and writing in "chat" mode, creating signs and while creating command blocks, which is the programming language of Minecraft. Children naturally challenge each other in terms of vocabulary and comprehension. Unable to keep up with peers in "pick and peck" typing mode, everyone is motivated to learn basic keyboarding.

When you first start playing Minecraft, controlling the character with the Mouse and Keyboard might be challenging, but most kids are naturals. Keystrokes or movements quickly become innate. When they move forward in-game, they

aren't aware they are pressing precise key combinations, they simply think about moving forward and their hands do the rest.

On a social level, strict behavior guidelines and values of respect are reinforced at F2W. We have created a culture of positive communication and encourage the children by example. Children are divided into groups based on skill set and interest. For example, those most interested in engineering concepts and builds are naturally attracted to redstone. Peer mentoring happens quite naturally. Jenny had never used redstone to automate her creations. She was stumped when it came to the elevator in her home and lighting torches around the premises. Carl was quick to hop onto her computer and talk her through the steps while showing her.

Within days, Jenny mastered the basics of "electricity" and her designs became much more complex, much more interactive. Later, when studying about inventors at school, the inventions of Tesla came to life and Jenny not only wrote a report, but printed out some of her Minecraft inventions as examples.

We have been fortunate to partner with Stephen Fickas, Ph.D., Professor in the Department of Computer and Information Science at the University of Oregon. He and his team of graduate students and students designed an online store for F2W and other local programs. The inventory in this store falls into three categories, Virtual, Privilege or Tangible Product. Widgetarians earn points through exercise using Fitbits. The calories burned and recorded on the devices are converted into points that are then a part of the F2W economy. The F2W Store runs weekly or monthly specials. Each child has the opportunity to create a "wishlist" that is saved to their profile. When they have earned enough points to purchase something on their wishlist, they receive a notification. Children love it because it is fun and gives them an opportunity to earn real value items and shop. Parents love it because their children are moving and staying physically active. Professor Fickas talks a bit more about the store, and how a group or family can build their own store, in the **Poco Appendix**.

What has made our "Leap of Faith," so successful is responsive and engaged children enraptured by the magical world of Minecraft, parents who support their child's interest and other community partners

supporting our vision.

CHAPTER 5
What the Experts Say

Debra came up to the desk looking bleary-eyed. "I have a headache and feel nauseous," she reported. Immediately F2W staff began looking for a cause. How long had Debra been on the computer? A quick review of her attendance record indicated she had only been on-site 20 minutes. Phew! We were relieved. For as much as we love technology and advocate for all things technical, we too have concerns about too much screen time and childhood balance.

When it comes to research regarding the subject, you can find experts advocating both sides of the equation. That being said, we lean toward the wise use of technology, where children are encouraged to be creative, safe and self-disciplined. As it turns out, after encouraging Debra to drink a glass of water and stretch out, she remembered that she had forgotten to wear her glasses. A quick call home and the issue was resolved. If only all adult screen time concerns could be remedied so easily!

We've compiled some expert testimony regarding screen time, computer based learning and technology in general. We hope that this allays fears some of you may be having.

According to Eric Klopfer, Professor and the Director of the Massachusetts Institute of Technology's Scheller Teacher Education Program, "a study by S.R.I. International, a Silicon Valley research group that specializes in technology, found that game-based play could raise cognitive learning for students by as much as 12 percent and improve hand-eye coordination, problem-solving ability and memory."

"Games like Minecraft also encourage what researchers call 'parallel play,' where children are engrossed in their game but are still connected through a server or are sharing the same screen. And children who play games could even become better doctors. No joke. Neuroscientists performed a study at Iowa State University that found that surgeons performed better, and were more accurate on the operating table, when they regularly played

video games."

"Minecraft extends kids' spatial reasoning skills,

construction skills and understanding of planning,

said Professor Klopfer. In many ways, it's like a

digital version of Lego."[2]

A leading expert and blogger for Forbes Magazine,

Jordan Shapiro, weighs in on technology based

learning too. "'We're discussing whether it is a

good or bad thing whether people read on a screen

versus paper and they're going, [What? We're just

trying to get people to read. We don't care how,]

---

[2]By Nick Bilton, Disruptions: Minecraft an Obsession and an Educational Tool (New York Times Magazine, September 15, 2013)

Shapiro said... in a conversation with gamesandlearning.org."

"Since appearing at the Global Education and Skills Forum in Dubai last March, Jordan Shapiro, Forbes writer and Temple University professor, has been attending international conferences and has come away seeing games as a way to implement major educational reforms in many of these places."

"'The adoption is so easy and so cheap,'" Shapiro said of technology in education. "'If you suddenly read John Dewey on education and you wanted to institute Dewey's ideas across an entire nation, you are talking billions of dollars and probably 40 years of training before you have effectively made that transition. But you can have a game in every classroom next week.'"[3]

Jordan Shapiro is, by his definition,"a full-time father of two little boys. I teach in Temple University's Intellectual Heritage Department. I write regularly for Forbes, Mindshift KQED, HuffPo, and the Joan Ganz Cooney Center at Sesame Workshop. I speak internationally about edTech, game based learning, and 21st Century parenting. I hold a PhD in Depth Psychology, specializing in Jungian/archetypal psychology and phenomenology/Heideggerian philosophy. In particular, I study the ways video games (and other

---

[3] By Lee Banville, Shapiro: Games Could Be Powerful Leveler in Global Education (GamesAndLearning.Org, February 12, 2015)

new forms of interactive storytelling) teach us to make sense of the world."[4]

Dr. Shapiro authored the KQED, MindShift's Guide to Digital Games and Learning Series in 2014. It addresses parents and educators' questions about the role of digital games in learning. It is an excellent resource![5]

And this is just the beginning..."Digital game-based learning has come a long way, and many educators believe it is still an effective approach in teaching."

"Game-based learning is the educational strategy of taking something that many students know and love

---

[4] Jordan Shapiro (Forbes Magazine)

[5] By Jordan Shapiro, From Mars to Minecraft: Teachers Bring the Arcade to the Classroom (KQED News, July 10, 2014)

— video games — and translating it into a classroom activity. As more teachers adopt this strategy, students are getting the chance to play games of all types in the classroom, and the result is an informative lesson taught through a medium that students of all ages can connect with."

"Minecraft (Rated E 10+)

What it teaches: Digital Citizenship"

"According to one of the game's developers, Minecraft has sold 54 million copies, so it should be familiar to most students. Minecraft is an open-world, block-based adventure game, where players can explore, build, craft and fight monsters. Edutopia published a video that explores how this title can be used to teach digital citizenship, which includes Internet ethics and online safety and privacy."

"An in-game example of digital citizenship involves the concept of survival. Resources are important in Minecraft. Players need food to survive the wild, and materials to create tools and structures. One strategy for teaching digital citizenship with Minecraft is to help students understand that they need to ask permission before taking someone's materials or cooperate to produce the materials in the first place. The metaphor not only teaches the importance of cooperation but also can be used to educate students on the perils of plagiarizing."

"Andrew Miller, an educational consultant for Edutopia, listed several other strategies for using

Minecraft in education. One of his ideas allows students to explore locations, which they otherwise wouldn't be able to experience, through Minecraft (you can freely download maps that somebody else took the time to build). For example, students have the ability to take a virtual, pixilated tour of Shakespeare's Globe Theatre or the ancient Roman Coliseum."[6]

A local expert who we know, Peter Tromba, Research and Policy Director for the Oregon Education Investment Board, has first-hand knowledge of what it means to use Minecraft as a teaching tool. While serving as Principal of a middle school in Oregon, Tromba launched a pilot

---

[6] Kyle Rother, Video Games Are Playing a Pivotal Role in the Classroom (EdTechMagazine, July, 2014), k-12 article.

program where students used the game to meet common core standards in learning. He had students study the Oregon content standards and national curriculum resources to involve them in defending the use of the game for educational purposes. The results were engaged students and a waiting list of potential participants.[7]

"Patience, persistence and work are all attributes of Minecraft play," says <u>Extra Credits</u>, a YouTube Channel focused on gaming. It has many insightful videos. One in particular, <u>Extra Credits - How Minecraft Changes the Future of Games - Minecraft</u>

---

[7] Peter Tromba, Build Engagement and Knowledge One Block at a Time with Minecraft (Learning and Leading with Technology, June/July 2013)

Generation, is an exceptionally well done video exploring the video game design industry."[8]

Even the American Psychological Association has published regarding the learning, social and health benefits of video game play for kids.[9] Of course, every parent must decide for themselves what is appropriate for their unique child. There is a distinction between productive and unproductive screen time, casual learning and studying. Reading is no longer confined to paper books, digital books and coursework have been game changers. What are your beliefs and standards around the use of technology? The integration of video game play and

---

[8] Extra Credits YouTube Channel, https://www.youtube.com/watch?v=0K8G6BFg1Wk
[9] "The Benefits of Playing Video Games," Isabela Granic, PhD, Adam Lobel, PhD, and Rutger C.M.E. Engels, PhD, Radboud University Nijmegen; Nijmegen, The Netherlands; *American Psychologist*, Vol. 69, No. 1.

computer based learning requires that we make

intentional and thoughtful choices for our families.

The choices we make today are important, and with

the constant changes taking place ,those choices

will inevitably evolve.

CHAPTER 6
Your Child's Community and the Community of Mojang

Your child's community within the game of

Minecraft is a shared experience. You can achieve

more through cooperation than you can alone. The

creative aspect can be experienced alone or in

partnership. Fending off monsters, growing food

and mining for resources is easier when

accomplishing these feats with a friend. It's also

more FUN!

"Josh, is that your world?" Angie was incredulous.

"Yeah, I've been working on it a long time now.

Want to see my the tower I made?" Josh talked

easily to his friend without self-consciousness. One of the gifts of Minecraft is that it is a level playing field for all, regardless of gender. Within minutes, Josh had opened his world to LAN and Angie was teleported to his location. Moments later, six others were clamoring to join them.

"Creative or Survival?" someone could be heard asking.

"Are we doing PVP?" someone else chimed in.

"Wait, teleport me too," yet another asked.

We have heard concerned parents speak of too much screen time and the isolation of computer play. When it comes to Fidgets2Widgets' Education and the teaching tool of Minecraft, nothing could be further from the truth. Our employees complain about the noise levels in play and are shocked to hear the cacophony, the squeals of delight. Children excitedly talk, laugh, learn and share with each other. Those concerned parents, leave our premises reassured and informed by what they observe. Technology is the glue of our community and creates connection, not isolation. Minecraft servers allow players from all over the world to interact in game. Friendships are born and expertise is shared openly.

Although there are many servers out there, all servers are not created equal and they're not all appropriate for children. Because of its unprecedented popularity, Minecraft is played by young and old alike. Some families even play the game together now. Adults play and interact in ways that can include profanity on "chat" and more aggressive in-game play. Many servers advertise as family friendly, but there are no systems in place to ensure that those playing are truly children. We, at F2W, tested family servers repeatedly by submitting a "test" online registration, filled out by one of our 22-year-old employees. Within minutes access to the server was granted based only on an online application process. At F2W, we vet each and every distance learner by requiring a Skype interview. We can say, with certainty, that our server is a child only server. A closed server, we are not open to the general public and require membership through "whitelisting" in order to play.

Markus Persson created the game. Always a bit of a loner as a child, Markus learned to code at the early age of 8. He used a commodore 64 computer and from those humble beginnings, Minecraft was born.

Markus has always been committed to sharing his games freely. In fact, as the many incarnations of Minecraft took place, both Alpha and Beta versions, Markus allowed people opportunities to try it out and give feedback[10].

This feedback appeared in many forms. Initially, gamer forums sparked lots of conversation, but the conversation went viral when it hit YouTube.

YogsCast, TheDiamondMinecart, CaptainSparklez, TheBajanCanadian and Stampylongnose were some of the first and most popular YouTubers. Many started creating Minecraft videos for fun, but as

---

[10]By Ryan Mac, David M. Ewalt and Max Jedeur-Palmgren, Inside the Post-Minecraft Life of Billionaire Gamer... (Forbes Magazine, March 23, 2015)

popularity increased, found themselves working full time to produce more videos. More than one college student abandoned their studies, to pursue the entrepreneurial adventures in Minecraft. Big revenues have been generated through advertiser support.

Mojang, the developing company for Minecraft, has never been concerned with gamers or programmers who might want to enhance or change the game.

The coding is "open source," which means that it is not hidden or encrypted. Motivated individuals are welcome to take the original or "vanilla" version of Minecraft and modify it. There are platforms that then offer this modified version of the game in the form of ModPacks. Feed the Beast, ATL Launcher and Technic are some of the most popular platforms that offer scores of modded games. These mods are thematic in nature. For example, there is a Pokémon version of Minecraft where the basic version of the game has been modified to include many of the Pokémon characters and spells. Mods that are biome focused sport dinosaurs, pre-historic bugs, medieval themes, rainforests, tropics and MORE! If you can imagine it, most likely some modder has created it. There are aeronautic mods, railroad mods, engineering themes, wild west and cannon or TNT modified games. And even though kids love to try out various modded versions, they always come back to the simplicity, creativity and limitless potential of the vanilla version. Almost all of our curriculum is taught using this version of the game.

The open source environment of Minecraft encourages camaraderie in those who play. Gone is the temptation to crash or glitch the game and create mischief. You can channel any desire you have to manipulate or change the game quite honestly and without any major roadblocks other than needing to know how to code yourself. There are opportunities, however, to use JavaScript and Python languages to make changes.

Minecraft can be played on most cell phones or tablets (pocket edition) or on X-Box, iMac or PC. It is reasonably priced at under $30 to download the game and is a one-time only fee. Playing the game after download is always free. Servers and Modded sites make money through advertising, not by charging fees.

CHAPTER 7
Real World Applications

The real world applications of Minecraft play are many. It is more than a game. It is a resource-rich environment where high level reasoning and learning take place. For some, Minecraft is a gateway to coding, game making and making mods. This can easily lead to further study and potential careers in the computer sciences, engineering or architecture. Every university student intern we have had at Fidgets2Widgets, uses their experience playing Minecraft to talk with the kids intelligently about the game and the real world applications. Physics students talk about missiles and projectiles in motion to teach physics concepts.

Mathematicians use group builds as a teaching tool.
The kids are curious, challenged and then learn.
This happens organically and authentically as a part
of the experience itself. Unlike learning
environments that feel coercive or purposeless, kids
want to learn here. The result is the cultivation of
tenacity, focus and good study skills, without that
being the primary purpose or intention.

Electrical and mechanical engineering skills are learned using redstone, the wiring and circuitry tool in Minecraft. It is based on Binary Code and Logic Gates systems. These skill sets are used when creating machinery or industrial complexes. If you want to sample this, you can easily find videos on YouTube that will...BLOW YOUR MIND! These innovative creations use engineering, math and physics theories, while offering kids an opportunity to exercise critical thinking skills and experiment with hypotheses.

"In this image a player has created a 1 kilobyte Computer Hard Drive purely out of Redstone. Clever players can replicate almost any Computer System, referred to as algorithmic logic units. Your imagination really is the limit here. Professors have been known to use Minecraft for teaching lessons on Computer Logic.

One of the emerging fields of study is GIS or Geographic Information Systems. An employee and

Minecraft expert at F2W is pursuing a career in GIS. Minecraft, Portal2, and Kerbal Space Program are all games that foster interest in this area. They use complex maps, tracking systems and coordinates in gameplay and kids love it and learn it. It's like eating your spinach and LOVING it!

The creation of towns in various geographical locations and conditions is something most children experiment with. You can almost detect the future urban planners when you see the consternated child, feverishly rebuilding and redesigning a city that was destroyed by natural disasters, creepers or TNT. "Once burned, twice shy," these are the kids begging Max to "protect their city," with coding that renders their creations untouchable.

As we alluded to earlier, one of the fun and challenging aspects to the game are the lovable and dreaded creepers who like to destroy structures block by block. Michael had worked very hard on his village one day, only to return the next and find his house and neighborhood destroyed. Courageous and indomitable, he convinced his friends to help him rebuild, enticing them with the promise that Max would protect their village and it would be even better than the last. Max helped by providing rare building materials and the "build" was on.

The children that are attracted to Minecraft are typically quite self-reliant. They are seekers of information, self-starters and comfortable with research. They initiate expert Google searches without a second thought, are comfortable sleuthing that unusual video or tutorial on YouTube that is information rich. These children know their way around Wikipedia like nobody's business. Research and Development is second nature and helps prepare them for the natural integration of such skills in any job or career in R&D.

Artists are attracted to the creativity of the game, as well as the artistry of biomes, skins and architecture. In short, Minecraft offers something to everyone as evidenced by its mass appeal to all interests.

If you as a parent want to motivate your child, Minecraft affords a myriad of opportunities to do just that. A child who is motivated and challenged, allowing their innate curiosity to fuel their interests, will most certainly use these skills in their future career. If your child is obsessed with Minecraft, that's a very good sign!

CHAPTER 8

Minecraft Mania

"Alex, Alex?"

"I thought you were going to open to LAN.What's the IP?? K, now I'm on, but I need you to TP me. Are cheats on?Where are you?Where are you?Guys, guys.Somebody come help me farm this Iron.Did somebody spam cows, because they are

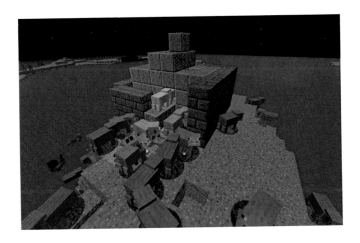

everywhere, I can't see. Where is the glowstone?

Mobs are spawning in my house!"

Need a translator? Alex wanted to play with his
friends on a Local Area Network (LAN)
connection. Once he is told what the LAN is, he
needs the owner of the world to teleport (TP) him,
with a command, to where the group of friends are
playing. There was a bountiful harvest of Iron Ore
and 'Farming' is the systematic gathering of
resources, not just plant crops . He wasn't aware
that yes, someone had indeed spammed (created and
duplicated in excess) some cows in order to get
steaks. But just after Alex entered the world and
was teleported, night fell and he was blind.
Glowstone or torches provide light to see and that
was what he was looking for, but just at that

moment, he was surrounded by creepers (Mobs spawn naturally in the dark).

Minecraft jargon was born out of necessity. There are so many concepts and ideas that it can become tedious explaining certain things. "Let's efficiently gather a large amount of pork right now" becomes "let's farm some pork". "Someone is spawning cows way too fast, there's no need for that many, please stop" becomes "Please stop spamming cows!". "We should build a house that doesn't allow monsters to come inside and keeps us safe at night" becomes "Let's Mob-Proof our base."

When we grew up, it was common for us to speak pig-latin with our friends, as our own secret "kid" language. That language was easy and involved taking the first letter of a word and adding it to the end of the word with an "a". So, the word "candle" would be pronounced "andle-ca." Today, kids speak Minecraft. It is a rich language filled with unique in-game adjectives, nouns and verbs. And it already influences how the world talks. We speak of mining and spawning and "tp-ing" and taming...all Minecraft activities.

Whenever our society begins to move too far in any direction, culture has a way of helping restore the balance. Modern education, city living and fears involving the dangers of the world at large, have changed the way we parent. Children's lives are as scheduled as their adult counterparts. Rather than relying on the authentic, imaginative play of childhood to teach children what they need to learn, children are expected to pursue adult sized hobbies with tutors, instructors, experts or coaches. This learning, organized by the adults, does not appeal to the free flowing, imaginative, non-linear world of the child. When children bring this free flowing energy to piano, flute, soccer or spanish lessons, power struggles ensue and learning is stymied. Parents have known this at some level, but have felt confused or powerless to change what is.

Fastforward a few years to Minecraft and the *"mania"* makes perfect sense! Children who are no longer free to roam the neighborhoods unsupervised, build forts and treehouses, play war games or house, dig in the mud and climb trees, can now do these very things in Minecraft! Not only that, but they get to do it unsupervised (by and large) without fears of getting hurt or stranger danger. The joys of childhood have returned. You can dig in the mud and find treasure. You can make caves and encounter imaginary enemies, you can chop down trees, build fires, swim unattended, eat wild foods, tame wild animals, build your own fort or house, plant foods that grow quickly and give you health. This is an exciting world that feels real, but is still very much pretend.

Is it any wonder that when this game hit the Internet, the world went wild? The safety and innocence of childhood had returned. Even adults were captivated. They too were reminded of what it feels like to play in a world where you are powerful, not powerless, a world where there are limitless possibilities, joy, treasure and challenges around

every corner.

CHAPTER 9

A Mother's Ode to Minecraft by: MaryJo McLaughlin

My children have been playing Minecraft for three years now, but really, it's hard to recall the time when it wasn't a part of their lives. From the beginning, it was clear that this wasn't your average video game. They loved my iPhone and fought each other to play various games but none captured their imagination or raised the level of competition for phone time like Minecraft. They were captivated. At that point, I didn't really get it, but I was tired of fighting to get my phone back, so I did what every parent seeking sanity would do, I bought them both their own PC Minecraft logons. Then it was "game-on" for them and for me. Finally, I got it.

A quick background on my kids, to help put my Minecraft experience in perspective; I have a 12 year old son, Kieran and a 10 year old daughter, Kate.

Kieran has Asperger's, although he's always been in a regular classroom. He's extremely bright with an excellent sense of humor. He's never met a pun he didn't love. He excels at school academically and although he struggles to make a true friend, his easy manner, quick wit, and honesty make him a favorite among his classmates. He approaches life without an agenda (other than how to get more

Minecraft time) and I don't know if he's ever doubted himself once in his 12 years.

Kate is also very, very bright, although in an unassuming way. She loves to be the center of attention on her own terms, has an above average social intelligence and a reading level and vocabulary well beyond her years. She moves easily between social groups and is a friend to many. She has a great sense of humor, but it's hard to make her truly laugh. When it happens, you know you've struck gold, it's special.

It's easy to identify the very basic skills my kids gained from playing PC Minecraft at the ages of 7 and 9; improved keyboarding and use of the mouse, navigating the web, establishing and remembering log-ons and passwords and of course, the importance of being safe on the internet. But, these are skills any online game can provide. When I witnessed firsthand, the two of them thinking spatially, understanding that height, width and depth create volume and conceptualizing scale and proportion, I started to realize the game adds real world value. As they've played more and more, they've gained and understanding of basic electrical circuits and coding skills But even all that comes nowhere close to understanding what Minecraft really did, and still does for my kids.

Minecraft is a vehicle for understanding the creative process. It lets them create what they want, when they want and how they want with the only boundary being bedtime (or equivalent parent determined end time). When they were first learning the game and the mining, crafting and brewing rules, I'd give them "quick build" assignments. They "built" houses, schools, businesses etc. Then they had to tell me what they built and what inspired them to choose what they did. They pushed each other to raise the bar each time. And I gained insight into my kids' minds and how they see the world and their place in it.

Minecraft teaches resourcefulness. They play on servers on survival mode. If they want to stay in the game, they have to manage their health and hunger. They've learned how to make good choices and the consequences of bad choices. For Kieran especially, this has been very positive. As a kid with Asperger's, it's often hard for him to focus on what's important. There's so much stimulation everywhere in the world, it can be hard to block out the minutiae. He's learned the consequences of paying attention to a benign mob, only to be undone by a hostile one. It's a lesson he's learning to apply to life, especially now, as the distractions of middle school mount.

Minecraft gives kids control and freedom at the same time. I notice this especially with my daughter. She builds neighborhoods and communities exactly how she wants them. From the design of the houses to the inclusion of the types of vehicles, businesses and recreational venues; it's all Kate. Her houses are artistic yet pragmatic, like she is. She's a student of life's details, which becomes obvious when you study what she creates.

Kate's true passion in life is food. Not just eating it, but learning about ingredients, cooking processes and nutritional value. When it comes to food, Kate has a never ending sense of adventure. But unfortunately, for a 10 year old girl, who's the tallest kid in the class, and challenged at shedding her baby fat, an interest in food is often regarded as a negative. Thank goodness for Minecraft, it gives her the freedom to engage in what she loves, without judgment. She designs restaurants of all types; sit down, drive thru, buffet - you name it. She includes menu boards and utilizes all the resources Minecraft has to offer. She thinks of every detail whether it be the hostess stand, the countertop cash register or the table sizes and number of seats. It's where Kate is her most expressive self. She takes pride in showing me what she's made, what she was thinking and telling me how someday she'll have her own restaurant.

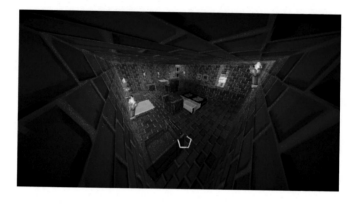

Minecraft lets kids be heroes or villains. I notice this with my son, Kieran. He's a sweet and gentle boy, with a dark side. He loves to be vengeful and has a passionate desire to win at all costs. He won't think twice about stealing your resources or using his diamond sword enchanted with fire aspect to send you to your doom. In his everyday life, he's easy going and wouldn't hurt anyone or anything on purpose. But consider yourself warned: if you end up in the same survival game as him, you're going down and he's not saying "sorry". More than anything Kieran wants to host a game server. I told him I'll look into it, but he has to create an original game; no stealing someone's hard work. As such, he's spent many hours so far writing ideas for maps, kits and levels and whatever else he needs. He's focused and determined to make it a reality. Of course, like his love of being the villain, it's dark and probably a little disturbing to those who don't know him. I, however, am glad he has a safe medium, in which to express his dark side safely. To me, it's no different than a horror novelist or movie maker.

Minecraft provides community. Whether it's playing online PVP games or at Fidgets2Widgets*, playing Minecraft provides my children the opportunity to meet other kids. Some are like-minded, some are not, some are on the other side of the world, some are across town; but no matter what, they all speak the same language. This spills over into non-Minecraft playing times, as well. My son has had numerous conversations with the siblings of his sister's basketball, softball and volleyball teammates. These are social interactions I absolutely guarantee wouldn't happen without the common interest and language of Minecraft. Even when my kids play together, they frequently teach and reinforce each other. Minecraft has strengthened their sibling bond.

And finally, Minecraft lets you watch football. I pride myself on being an active hands-on parent. From time to time I sit with my kids, watch them play and build. I ask them about what they're playing or building and have attempted to build my own world. I can even hold my own in Minecraft trivia to a point. I do this in an effort to understand what my kids love. My joy however is college football. I'm an avid fan living in a college town that's passionate about its team. If I'm not at the game, I'm watching on TV. On these occasions we have a little saying in my house – "no bones, no blood, no fire, no flood". It means you can play Minecraft until the cows come home, just don't break yourselves or the house. I'll be in the other room – watching football. I'm ok with that because

I know Minecraft gives as well as it gets and the entertainment it provides is not a one-sided experience.

*Side Note re: Fidgets2Widgets – A few years ago we went to Disneyland. If you've been there, or know anything about Disney, you know their tag line is it's the "happiest place on Earth". Kieran, my very literal son, was concerned that the Disney Company was lying. He told me point blank, without meaning to be funny that "Disney is NOT the happiest place on earth, Fidgets2Widgets is."

Poco Appendix

Hi. I'm Steve Fickas. I lead the group that built the store for Fidgets2Widgets. We call the store Poco. We have been so pleased with its operation, we decided to make it available more widely. If you are interested in building your own Poco store, for your school, for your group, even for your family, please drop me a line. You can email me at Fickas@cs.uoregon.edu Thanks!

Sydney Ashland, Founder

Sydney Ashland has worked as a consultant with children for over 17 years. During this time she developed, in collaboration with Pam Simon, a child development theory based on elemental laws. Her work has been highly effective with children suffering from the effects of ADHD, ADD and sensory integration issues. Creator/Author, <u>Childhood Energetics, Understanding our 21st Century Children</u>.

s.ashland@fidgets2widgets.com

Pam Simon, Founder

Pam Simon, L.M.S.W. has a Bachelors Degree in Speech Pathology and Audiology from the University of Iowa and a Masters Degree in Social Work, acquired from Gallaudet University. She is fluent in American Sign Language, and has specialized in communication disorders with both children and adults. Having worked with autism and sensory integration issues, Pam helped develop the theory of F2W to aid in her continuing work with children. Certified Childhood Energetic Coach.

p.simon@fidgets2widgets.com

Max Fickas, Chief Gaming Officer

Max is an avid hiker, an expert in Google-fu and all things technological, and a patient role model for kids. As a part-time college student at the University of Oregon, Max has also received cybercamp certification in 3-D modeling, Game Design, Game Modding, PhotoShop, and more. Max is our Chief Gaming Officer.

m.fickas@fidgets2widgets.com

21642972R00069

Made in the USA
San Bernardino, CA
29 May 2015